To Norm

who understands
these things.

Talby

4/5/16

UNTALKABLE

by

Talby

ISBN 978-0-9968213-5-3

Web site, Blog and Feedback:
www.Untalkable.com

Cover photo taken by the author over
Utsalady Bay, Camano Island, Washington State

"By its very nature it

can't be talked about"

Author's Preface

"Untalkable" is a simple word and a simple idea, but it came out of a life full of searching and thinking. Ever since I can remember, I have been convinced that all paths lead to a common truth. We are all human after all, and our human truth should be equally valid for all of us. At the same time, from childhood I have had an occasional personal experience of a sensation that I could not put words to, that I could not even name. It came unbidden, but always left a deep impression. It was a personal connection to something "I know not what," something that came out of the simple fact that I was alive and I was human.

I looked all over for some teaching that would help me put words to what I was experiencing and thinking, but nothing seemed to hit home. Finally, I began to write down my own "Fresh Thoughts," as I called them, which in turn led to some promising ideas that I could express in condensed form. It started with the secret of Life in one page, which led to the secret of Life in half a page *"for lazy muggs like me,"* then a God for all humans in half-a-sentence, and finally the unifying aspect of the world in a single word: *Untalkable.* (The next step is *"enlightenment in half-a-word"*!)

But with Untalkable, I felt that the word and concept were potentially so important, so universally human, that it deserved a book of its own. Here is that book.

A. G. "Talby" Tramposch

CONTENTS

UNTALKABLE

UNTALKABLE

I. Something There Is That Can't Be Talked About

We humans love to talk. We will talk to just about anyone, anywhere, about most anything. Being more talkative than wise, we might even go so far as to call ourselves *Homo gabulus.* In fact, we love to talk so much that we can't even conceive of something that can't be talked about.

Yet for as long as we can remember, we talkative humans have had a fascination with a part of the natural world that can't be described or put into words. In religion it's the "ineffable God," in philosophy the "truth behind concepts." Spiritual paths seek the "oneness beyond," psychology has the "collective unconscious," and artistic inspiration arrives unbidden from "we know not where." Even rational science looks for

1

"dark matter," logical mathematics requires illogical "infinity," and practical economics depends on the "invisible hand"—we can't say what these are, but we know they must exist because of their effects.

So it seems that nearly every field of human endeavor has its own way of talking about this part of the world, which emphasizes that it can't be described in words. And there's the rub. We acknowledge that this important aspect can't be talked about, but we seem to want to keep on talking about it. It's just too important to ignore. And we hope against hope that one day we will succeed in finding the right way to describe it, in writings, in explanations, in descriptions—in short, in words.

UNTALKABLE

Unfortunately, all our talking has not relieved us of the vague sense that what is being talked about does not exactly reflect what we ourselves are experiencing; of the feeling that there is something else that we are missing, something right in front of us that we can't quite grasp.

UNTALKABLE

Caught on the horns

So we are caught on the horns of a great metaphysical dilemma. When dealing with this aspect of the world, we seem to have only two imperfect options. The first option is to be absolutely silent about it. Legends tell us that the greatest sages in history are completely unknown. I believe this is because they knew this aspect of the world could not be talked about, and they were content to live out their lives not saying anything about it. But it is so important that the rest of us want to know about it too. If no one talks about it, that leaves us in ignorance. And if the secrecy becomes more important than the nature of the reality, then we are really out of luck.

The second option, if we do decide to share it, is to talk about it in vague metaphorical terms—spiritual, religious, or even poetic. One might do this, for example, to make others aware of how important it is, and to inspire us to become aware of it ourselves. This has worked up to a point. But talking about what can't be talked about changes it from what it actually is. And, being *H. gabulus*, we can easily get hooked on the words themselves. We fill libraries and bookstores, and pretty soon the words become more familiar, and more important, than the reality. In a way, the words become the reality for us. And if we become attached to the words that we are using in preference to the words used by others, this can divide us and lead to conflict.

Neither of these have turned out to be very good options.

Having it both ways

What if we could have it both ways? What if we could use *words themselves* to say that this aspect of the world is important and that it cannot be talked about, without actually talking about it? And what if the "something more that we are missing" is as simple as the realization that it is right here in our grasp, but we just can't talk about it?

This book suggests such an innovation: a way of using words themselves, or one word in particular, to refer to the unifying aspect of the world that can't be talked about, while at the same time not talking about it. Thus, it is not just another book that tries to talk about "what can't be talked about." Rather, it is a book about *how not to talk about what can't be talked about.*

Which is not as easy as it sounds!

The Word "Untalkable"

If there is an aspect of the world, or an aspect of our awareness of the world, that can't be talked about, why hasn't anyone figured out by now a way to refer to it without trying to describe or define it? In other words, why isn't there a word for something that can't be talked about, that does not itself amount to talking about it? Well, it turns out that there is.

Definition of "Untalkable"

The dictionary has a word for the things of the world that *can* be talked about. This word is "talkable," which means "capable of being talked about." And there is also a word in the dictionary, one which is almost never used, for the other aspect of the world, the aspect that *cannot* be talked about. This word is "Untalkable."

UNTALKABLE

The dictionary definition of "Untalkable" is, simply, "cannot be talked about." We might refine that just a little bit to say, "By its very nature it cannot be talked about." The word hasn't been used very much before, so it doesn't carry additional meanings from common usage to confuse us. And it seems familiar because it uses English roots, and we immediately have a sense of what it means.

Thus, Untalkable is an ideal word for the aspect of the world that we can experience, but by its very nature can't be talked about. And as we get used to this new word, we might get more and more used to the new concept, and how it might impact us and our lives.

What Can We Possibly Say About "What Can't Be Talked About?"

We of course can't say anything about Untalkable, since it can't be talked about. Not to others. Not even to ourselves. Fortunately, that doesn't mean that we can't say anything at all.

First, we can talk about what it is not. By looking at what Untalkable isn't, we might get a little better sense of what it might be.

Second, we can talk about human awareness. Just because Untalkable cannot be talked about, that doesn't mean that it can't be experienced. We might even suggest some exercises to encourage awareness of Untalkable.

Third, we can talk about how not to talk about it. This has been very difficult for us humans over the centuries, and in a way it has been the key difficulty. We can easily be aware of Untalkable, but once we are aware of it we invariably get skewered on the dilemma of either being completely silent about it, or talking about it in ways that change our awareness of it into something that it is not. Thus, we will talk about the difficult art of not talking about what can't be talked about, even after experiencing it.

Finally, we can talk about the possible effects and benefits of Untalkable. There are many things in the world that we cannot say anything about, but which have very practical effects on us and on our lives. Untalkable is one of these, and we can look at what some of the effects and benefits of Untalkable might be.

II. Talking About What It Is Not

While we cannot say anything directly about Untalkable, looking at "what Untalkable is not" might help us better understand what it might be.

We already know, of course, that Untalkable is not talkable: it can't be talked about.

> *Untalkable is not what we mean by other words we already know*

Another thing Untalkable is not: it is not what we are referring to when we use similar words, words we might otherwise prefer to use because we are more familiar with them, because they refer to things we already know.

For example, Untalkable does not mean silent, wordless or "beyond words." There are plenty of things that are silent, but can still be talked

about: sunsets, paintings, pantomime, dance. Other things like music are wordless but can be talked about: it is loud, melodic, *cool*. Untalkable isn't always silent. Silence isn't always Untalkable. And even talking can have an Untalkable aspect—think of a deeply moving prayer, poem or song.

Untalkable is not what we mean when we use words like unspeakable, inexpressible or indescribable. These refer to an excess of emotion that is hard but not impossible to put into words. Horror can be unspeakable, beauty can be inexpressible, joy can be indescribable, but these all can be talked about. Untalkable is also not unknown, unknowable or ineffable. We experience this aspect of reality from birth, and we live with it every day. Once we allow ourselves to be aware of it, we may be amazed at how familiar it seems.

Untalkable is not visible or invisible, it's not material or non-material. These are all ways of talking about it. Untalkable cannot be talked about, and that is all we can possibly say about it.

> *Untalkable is not God; but God may have an Untalkable aspect*

We might think at first that Untalkable refers to "God," or to the ultimate reality however we conceive it. True, it is hard to reduce "God" to words. But Untalkable is not what we are referring to when we use words such as "God." Our concept of God has some very specific qualities that we can talk about—absolute, all-knowing, omnipotent, merciful, creator. These are "talkable" aspects.

Yet I believe that everything, including God, has an Untalkable aspect. While some

qualities of God are known, others can't be talked about or described. If we could allow for this Untalkable aspect of God alongside the talkable aspects we already know, this might advance our understanding of our own beliefs, and perhaps even provide a bridge between different religions, and between religion and other forms of belief.[1]

* * *

Thus, we see that Untalkable is not any of the things we already know that can be talked about or described. It is, simply, that which by its very nature cannot be talked about. Anything else is not Untalkable.

---

[1] In the same way, the part of ourselves that we refer to as "soul" can be talkable to the extent we can say things about it, but it also has an Untalkable aspect.

III. Human Awareness
Of Untalkable

We humans are already aware of Untalkable in one way or another. Up to now, much of this awareness has come through words, which of course can't describe this aspect of reality. But the words can point in its direction. They can inspire us to become more aware of Untalkable, maybe even to open up to it. The words can be valid as a kind of "indirect awareness" of Untalkable, an affirmation that it exists and that it should be important to us. But we humans are also capable of more. We are capable of direct awareness of Untalkable.

Many of us have had spontaneous deep and moving experiences that we just can't put into words. These may well be direct experiences of Untalkable. I believe that our direct awareness of Untalkable is not limited to such

exceptional and random occasions. Rather, I believe that we can experience Untalkable very often. We can even be aware of it during our common daily activities and using our everyday consciousness, the same consciousness we use for taking out the trash and feeding the kids. We may not talk much about these modest experiences though, because, well, because we just *can't*. They are Untalkable. But we do have them. All of us.[2]

We of course will always be able to follow the more complex paths to deep spiritual experience. But through Untalkable we also have an alternative, moderate path, one that makes the experience available to many more people than before. This moderate path can

---

[2] Little children especially seem to swim joyfully in a sea of Untalkable.

allow us to seek the experience and the reality, while remaining grounded in our family, friends, career, hobbies and beliefs.[3]

---

[3] It is usually thought that traditional paths are complex and difficult in order to overcome significant obstacles to awareness of what can't be talked about. But it could also be the other way around; it could be that we can experience Untalkable rather easily, and the complex teachings are meant to train us in the difficult task of not talking about it even after experiencing it. If so, the word Untalkable can help make this relatively easy. *See* Chapter IV, below.

Achieving Direct Awareness

The first step to become aware of Untalkable is to realize that it exists, and that we can be aware of it. The second step is to actually become aware of it; to cultivate daily awareness of Untalkable. This section sets out a few easy-to-do exercises that can help open us up to that awareness.

Before doing these exercises, you might like to read the initial chapters once again. They will seem totally different the second time through. That's just how our minds work—the first time is to set a foundation, and the second is for more complete understanding.

UNTALKABLE

Also dwell gently on the word "Untalkable." Remind yourself of the word a couple of times a day, perhaps putting one-word notes by the bedside, on a wristband or refrigerator magnet, or leaving this book where you can see it. Let the word become familiar and the meaning sink in, and let awareness of Untalkable open up naturally.

Exercises For Direct Awareness

The point of the following exercises is to demonstrate to ourselves that Untalkable is not just an abstract concept, and to set us on the path of opening our daily awareness to it. Don't expect the new awareness to be different than daily life. It will be exactly like daily consciousness, just Untalkable. You will be aware of it, but you won't be able to describe it. Don't try. And don't worry about the words in your mind, don't try to get rid of them. Simply be aware of Untalkable that exists at the same time.

For each exercise, you can time it with your breaths. Breathe a couple of times. Then a handful of times. Let it go at that.

UNTALKABLE

Exercise 1: Hands

Hold your hands palms facing forward. Your arms can be in any position. I don't know why this works, but it does.

Exercise 2. Awareness of Untalkable in and around you

Imagine yourself inside a hollow sphere of awareness. Be aware of the entire surface of the sphere at once.

To help with this, simultaneously notice the six points on the sphere corresponding to up, down, left, right, forward, back. Or picture yourself in a cube, and simultaneously notice the eight corners. Or be in a room, and notice the ceiling, floor and four walls, or the eight corners. Or lie under the night sky and be aware of all the stars at once, in both the northern and southern hemispheres. Or be in the middle of a flock of birds, fluttering all around. Or be at the center of a globe, and be aware of all the oceans and continents at once.

UNTALKABLE

Think of something attractive that naturally draws your attention, and imagine it behind you; be aware of everything in front of you, and of that very appealing thing behind you, all at the same time. The important thing is to be aware of all directions at once.[4]

Do this one or two times a day, while breathing a few breaths. When you are comfortable in the sphere, let the sphere become filled with awareness. Let the awareness fill your body, and all around it. Let it be like a cloud of Untalkable.

---

[4] I particularly like this concept of "spherical awareness." We all think of comprehensive awareness as "360 degrees." But 360° only represents the circumference of a circle in two dimensions. Our everyday human consciousness is three dimensional; it is spherical, like being inside a globe of awareness. To show how much greater our spherical awareness is than 360°, the surface of a sphere contains no less than 41,253 "square degrees."

Exercise 3. Awareness of Untalkable in others

After you become aware of the cloud of Untalkable around yourself, be aware of it when someone else is there. It can be friend, family or stranger. You don't have to tell them what you are doing.

When you are comfortable with that, be aware of a sphere of awareness around the other person. Then be aware of the two spheres or clouds communicating or overlapping. Then be aware of your body and the other person's body within a single larger cloud. Don't get physically closer to the other person, do this simply with your imagination and awareness.

Exercise 4. Working with a partner

If you are working with a partner, sit and hold hands and be aware of each other and the cloud of Untalkable at the same time. Let your clouds overlap if they want to. Be both inside the same cloud if that feels comfortable. Feel the love and connection that is generated by this awareness.

Lie still on your partner's back, with your heads close together. Only do this if health, comfort and propriety permit. "Spooning" can work too, but there is something about the feeling of weight that seems to make a difference.

Remind each other during the day of Untalkable, of your Untalkable connection to each other, and how you experience it in your daily life.

Exercise 5. Awareness of Untalkable in the world around you

Be aware of your sphere. Let it fill the room. Let it fill the space between you and whatever is around you.

Pick a friendly place. Sit and imagine that you are not there. Let the "currents" and energy of the place (room, yard, woods, seashore) be the same as they would be if you were not there. Don't try to change what is around you; let your energy adapt to imitate the energies of the place.

Exercise 6. Prayer and meditation

During your usual prayer or meditation, be aware of Untalkable. Let that awareness deepen your experience, let it connect you to the reality you are seeking, let it gently bring you closer to it.

Be aware of the feeling-state inside you during prayer and meditation. Hold that Untalkable feeling within you in your daily life. Live your life a prayer.

If you don't pray or meditate, let your awareness of Untalkable be your connection to others, to the world, and to the unifying reality.

Exercise 7. Gratitude and Appreciation

A generalized feeling of gratitude or appreciation, and similar feelings, can help open us up to Untalkable. You can start by thinking of the things you are grateful for, the things that you appreciate.

But as soon as you can, let go of the list and just experience a feeling of deep gratitude and appreciation. Carry this feeling into your daily life.

Exercise 8. Direct awareness of the unifying aspect of reality

While being aware of Untalkable, dwell on the possibility of an aspect of the world that we cannot talk about, that is the same for everyone. Open to that unifying aspect, a love that is unity and harmony. Let it bring you closer to others of all beliefs, to the world around you, and to the ultimate reality however you conceive it.

If you are scientifically oriented, be aware of the Untalkable energy that exists in atomic and sub-atomic particles, in light, in the elements, in energy, in gravity. Imagine Untalkable pervading space. Let the Untalkable aspect of quantum reality gently reveal itself to you.

Exercise 9: Laughing

I'm in a quandary whether to be in awe of Untalkable, or to just sit back and have a good laugh. The answer may be that laughter can help us feel awe at Untalkable, while not having to talk about it.

Some yogis say that the best meditation is to laugh—just to laugh, to laugh at nothing. Try saying the word Untalkable out loud a couple of times a day, when you think of it. It just might make you laugh—*to laugh at nothing!*[5]

---

[5] On my better days, I can't even get out all full four syllables without breaking into a belly-laugh!

Final Exercise: Throw this darn book out, once you are done with it!

By all means unload this book as soon as you can, since it's full of *talking!* Better yet, give it to a friend.

Keep only the word and concept "Untalkable," and go about your daily life with a new awareness of that marvelous aspect of the world and of yourself!

UNTALKABLE

* * *

These gentle exercises may give us an idea of what awareness of Untalkable might be like. There are many other ways that we can open up to it. Use any of them that you want, or make up your own. Keep opening up awareness at new times, in new places, with new people. Encourage others to develop their own awareness, reminding each other always that Untalkable cannot be talked about.

IV. How Not To Talk About Untalkable, Even After Experiencing It

So we are all capable of having experiences that we can't find words for. But once we have experienced it, what is it that we have experienced? It is so tempting to speculate about what it is, to compare it to things we have heard about, to put it into "context." We want to share it with others, we want to feel good about it and about ourselves, we want to understand how it changes or deepens our place in the world and our relation to the greater reality.

Unfortunately, all of this requires words. And the very act of talking about the experience can turn it into something other than what it is. Talked about, even in retrospect, it is no longer an Untalkable experience. It becomes something talkable, something that is

different than the experience itself. It may even become something that never existed at all. Except, of course. in words.

So once we have experienced it, how can we know what it is that we have experienced? That's just the point—we can't answer this question. We can't say anything about what it is; we simply can't talk about it, either to ourselves or to others. Once we experience Untalkable, it is the hardest thing imaginable not to try to explain it. How can we avoid trying to say what it is or what it might be, somehow putting words to it, somehow talking about it?

Up to now, we haven't had the right tools to help us experience this part of reality, and then incorporate it smoothly into our belief system, our daily lives, our relationships, our self-image and our worldview, all without

putting it into words. What we need is something that can help us achieve the experience, and then practice not talking about what can't be talked about.

Seeking The Experience Without Talking About It

As we seek these deeper experiences, the word Untalkable itself can help guide us to it in a way that we know ahead of time it can't be talked about. The word becomes a kind of invitation and inspiration to that aspect of reality, while warning us that there will be no words to describe it. We may then be able to approach it with a minimum of expectations, and with a more open heart and mind. The resulting experience may be of a moderate and manageable kind, one that enhances our lives and deepens our understanding of ourselves while not separating us from others.

Sharing And Validating A Personal Experience

As we have seen, neither silence nor talking are very good options once we have had such an experience. What we really need is a convenient way to refer to the experience, while reminding ourselves, our friends and our loved ones that we cannot talk about it. The word Untalkable allows us to seamlessly integrate the experience into our talking lives, and at the same time avoid talking about it. We won't make the mistake of distorting the experience by putting words to it, and we won't feel the need to hide it from others even though it is very important to us, and presumably to them as well. With the word Untalkable, we can safely tell others that we had an "Untalkable experience," while steadfastly and respectfully refusing to talk

about it. They will respect that in return, and may simply respond, *"Wow. Cool. Me, too."*

In addition, we will no longer feel the need to validate or justify our experience through words, which can cause all sorts of difficulties. Since we now know that it is a common thing for humans to have such experiences, the word Untalkable by itself is enough to validate the experience, and this problem disappears. Using the word Untalkable, the experience remains pure experience.

Reminding Ourselves Not To Talk About It

Best of all, the very word Untalkable is an effective tool to help us achieve these goals, of avoiding the temptation to talk about our experiences, from overexcitement, or from a natural desire for understanding, communication and sharing.

If we use the word Untalkable for the experience, we won't need to describe it, to explain what it means, or to decide what we should do about it or because of it. The word itself reminds us there is nothing we can say about it. I am quite sure if we used any other word than Untalkable, something more poetic or spiritual-sounding for example, we would just end up talking about it. We couldn't help ourselves.

UNTALKABLE

* * *

So the word Untalkable helps us recognize that there is an aspect of the world that can't be talked about, and invites us to be aware of it every day without talking about it. It allows us to share our experience with others without having to describe it to them, and it validates the experience without the need to put words to it. Best of all, it serves as a constant reminder not to try to talk about it, or to let others "explain" it to us.[6] "Untalkable" is a one-word inspiration, communication, validation and reminder. It is absurdly convenient, and well-nigh foolproof.

---

[6] I have even been guilty of this myself: "Oh, you had an experience you can't put into words? Wow! *Let me tell you about a book I'm writing, that explains......*"

UNTALKABLE

Over time we can use the word to accustom our minds to accept that there is something, an aspect of the world and of ourselves, that by its very nature cannot be talked about. Not by you, by me, or by the greatest literary, spiritual or scientific geniuses. Not by saints, by poets, by linguists, by songwriters or by lovers. Not now, not soon, not ever. We may come up with beautiful language that sounds like it ought to mean something; we may fascinate each other with images that overwhelm our reason and our power to resist. But whatever we come up with, we still can't talk about Untalkable. Not because we aren't smart enough or talented enough or spiritual enough. But because it simply cannot be done.

Untalkable is *Untalkable*, and there's the end of it.

V. Possible Effects And Benefits
Of Untalkable

The final thing that we can talk about are the possible effects of Untalkable. We know there are things in the world that we cannot say anything about, for example, dark matter in physics, infinity in mathematics, the "invisible hand" in economics. But we can know them by their effects, which are measurable and point to their existence. Further, they are necessary in order that everything else makes sense. They "fill in the gaps" and allow the overall system to work. Perhaps Untalkable is like this as well. Perhaps Untalkable is necessary if our world is to make sense to us. And perhaps we can know it by its effects.

The Unifying Effect of Untalkable

The effect that actually led me to Untalkable in the first place, is that it is what connects us with other people and with the world around us. There are many things that are common to us as humans, and there are many differences. The one thing that cuts through all the commonalities and all the differences is Untalkable. Further, Untalkable is additive to our current beliefs, and non-intrusive to our way of life. This is because, not using words, it is compatible with each and every belief, and each and every way of living.

I do believe that Untalkable is a common aspect that we all share. Becoming aware of it in ourselves and in others can bind us together in, well, in an Untalkable way. In a certain sense, all human beliefs use words to refer to what can't be talked about. While these words have different meanings for different people,

UNTALKABLE

Untalkable has one and only one meaning. It is the same for everyone; a common aspect of every belief. It could serve as a language that all beliefs can recognize, and thus can create a bridge for understanding and acceptance among cultures and religions, and even between believers and non-believers.

A Practical Spirituality For Our Modern Culture

We live in an extraordinary time. It is like nothing we know has ever existed before. Our understanding of how the physical world works is broad and deep, and our practical awareness seems to touch on everything. Communications, information, technology, travel, education have all blossomed. Individual thought and freedom of action have kept pace to a large extent. But one thing that does not seem to have kept up is our human spirituality.

UNTALKABLE

Could Untalkable represent a practical spirituality for our modern culture?

Our spirituality should be equal to the time we live in. As we seek to experience and understand the "deeper" aspects of reality, many of us prefer to follow our own way of thinking and of searching. We don't want to have to ignore what we know about the world, the evidence of our life experiences, our education, or the intelligent opinions of our co-humans. Rather, we want to go about our quest within the context of our knowledge, our wisdom, and our own lives. And we certainly don't want to have to separate ourselves from family and friends, career, colleagues or social interests in order to pursue it.

Untalkable might be able to help us achieve all of these wonderful things. Because it has no words, it could be equally available to everyone, and could interlace smoothly with all worldviews from the great world religions, to philosophy and science, to alternative spiritual paths, to agnosticism and even atheism. And it can make perfect sense standing on its own and by itself, in the context of our lives and our personal searching. Perhaps the uniqueness and flexibility of Untalkable can help us build a useful, practical spirituality that fits our modern culture. Here are some examples.

UNTALKABLE

Untalkable and Religion

It stands to reason that every religion has an Untalkable aspect. Religion naturally tries to "talk about" what can't be talked about—that's what makes it a religion in the first place. We might think of religion as a kind of indirect awareness of Untalkable, a representation in words of what cannot be talked about for the purpose of pointing us to it and inspiring us to become aware of it. Religion is remarkable and wonderful in many ways, and it is something that we naturally hold to, because of its deep benefits from both personal and social perspectives.

Untalkable can be a tool to help us deepen our understanding and belief in our own religion, make it more meaningful and relevant to our lives, and allow us to relate to others whose beliefs might differ from our own. It does this

by simply reminding us that words cannot replace reality, that talking about what can't be talked about should not take precedence over the Untalkable reality itself. Thus the reality and the experience remain at the core of our religious belief, and the words we use are seen as supports and inspirations for our direct relation to the reality, rather than replacements for them. The great value of Untalkable is that it can fit comfortably in this way with all religions, because it doesn't have any doctrines, tenets or dogmas of its own.

Untalkable and Science

Many of us who respect science still believe (or would like to be able to believe) that there is more to the world and to human life than what can be measured. But it may not feel right for us to hold to a practical-scientific reality on the one hand, and a separate and different religious-spiritual reality on the other. Wouldn't it be great if these two turned out to be a continuum, one seamless whole that could provide a coherent worldview for the full range of our humanity?

Untalkable might be such an approach. It can allow us to connect with the transcendent aspects of the world, while continuing to apply strict scientific observation and experimentation, and the rigorous logic that science requires.

UNTALKABLE

Untalkable and Spiritual Paths

Spiritual teachings often encourage us to put aside words in order to directly experience the "higher" realities. As we have seen, Untalkable can enrich our understanding of these teachings, and can enable us to incorporate them gracefully into our everyday lives. We can have the experiences we seek without feeling the need to attach unfamiliar words or concepts, which may distract our attention from the experiences themselves.

UNTALKABLE

Untalkable and non-spiritual philosophies

For those of us who hold to non-religious or non-spiritual philosophies, Untalkable might serve as a neutral reference to the deeper experiences of others, which these philosophies sometimes have difficulty explaining or incorporating. It can help us do that without getting bound up in arguments about words, and in this way it could provide a bridge between these philosophies and other religious and spiritual approaches.

UNTALKABLE

Untalkable as a stand-alone spirituality

Standing by itself, Untalkable can provide an admirable foundation for us as independent seekers. It can help us pursue our search while relying on our own thinking and our own guidance, allowing us to approach each step in a calm and balanced way. And as we become successful in experiencing the deeper realities, it can help us integrate our experiences without having to fall back on any existing philosophy, spiritual teaching or religion to give us a framework for relating to it.

And for folks who haven't yet put much of their attention to these "deeper" questions, Untalkable can be a simple and common-sense introduction to help understand what all this spiritual talk might be about, and to see how they could experience it in a safe and non-disruptive way.

UNTALKABLE

In these ways, and probably many more, Untalkable may lead us toward a practical spirituality for our modern world. As we seek the "deeper" and "higher" things of life, Untalkable may be a common sense way to encourage and inspire us in our quest; a way that can be non-intrusive, productive, harmonious and grounded. It is available equally to everyone, and may help us relate to each other, no matter what our background or beliefs. Best of all, it can leave room for our fundamental human practicality and wisdom, as we already know and practice them in our daily lives, and as we share them among ourselves—across cultures, across beliefs, and across boundaries of all kinds.

Other Possible Benefits

There are other possible benefits to using the word Untalkable, and to becoming aware of the aspect of the world that it refers to. Here are some examples of these.

A new dimension of awareness

First of all, Untalkable seems to be a significant aspect of the world and of our lives, so why not be aware of it? The concept Untalkable is almost ridiculously and embarrassingly simple. Even so, it can add a new dimension to our awareness with little or no effort or pain, without taking anything away from us, and without changing the things that we already know, experience and believe. It's kind of like winning a lottery that doesn't give us a lot of money to change our

life, but assigns someone to make every aspect of our current life better and more meaningful, without adding or subtracting anything.[7]

---

[7] It may even be that Untalkable *literally* refers to awareness of a "new dimension." We all know that separate objects can be connected in one higher dimension, like the puzzler of lifting a pencil up off the page to connect two dots without intersecting a line between them, or the cross-section of a 3-d doughnut appearing like two unconnected 2-d circles. Thus a higher dimension can have a kind of unity that is not apparent in the lower dimension. And it may stand to reason that the language of the lower dimension cannot express this reality and unity that exists only in the higher dimension. But this may be a discussion for another time, and another place!

.

UNTALKABLE

Awareness in our everyday mind

A major advantage of Untalkable is that it can be experienced in our everyday mind, without having to rely on unfamiliar concepts, strict practices or altered consciousness. This might be especially important for those who don't want their path to take them away from family, friends, career, or other aspects of their lives.

Further, we can understand the concept with our everyday minds, even without direct experience of Untalkable, and this itself may open us up to new possibilities and new thoughts.

UNTALKABLE

Reclaiming our lost beliefs

We've seen that Untalkable can deepen and lighten our current beliefs and experiences, freeing us to let them be just what they are without the need to explain them in words. In the same way, it might help reconcile us with the beliefs of our childhood that we may have left behind. If it could ease some of our conceptual doubts, it might open up a more universal relevance that we may not have seen before. It may allow us to see our childhood religion as one representation of this greater aspect of reality, and help us integrate it into our lives whether or not we return to it, while maintaining our individual thinking, experiences and convictions.

Relief!

As we stated at the beginning of our discussion, being aware of Untalkable can relieve us of that nagging voice in the back of our minds telling us "There's more to life than this. Get up and go find it!" By being aware of Untalkable, we might find that this "more to life" is already here and we already know it, if we would only stop trying to talk about it.

The Unidentified Source of Human Creativity

Untalkable can be a way of relating to the unidentified source of human creative inspiration. Great art, music, poetry, scientific inspiration and invention all seem to come from a place "we know not where." These great works can inspire us to become more aware of the Untalkable source of human creativity, and to be more creative ourselves.

UNTALKABLE

Adding the word to our vocabulary

I believe Untalkable has a deep and useful relevance even for those who don't believe that there is anything that can't be talked about. We don't live isolated in the world, and the beliefs of others are important to us, especially if we want to make progress in living together peacefully and in mutual respect. Untalkable can become a bridge of understanding, reframing the difference of beliefs in a simple and non-threatening way, and opening for us the possibility of mutual respect and acceptance, if not mutual belief. Even if it serves only as a placeholder to future knowledge, that in itself can have value. Adding the word to our modern vocabulary can provide a non-threatening way to allow for greater understanding, and new possibilities.

UNTALKABLE

* * *

Thus the word and concept Untalkable can have effects and benefits for our lives, our beliefs, and our relation to each other and to the world. And it might well represent the practical spirituality we are looking for in our modern culture. All this, without the need to adopt anything new, or let go of anything we already have. Untalkable is, in a way, an ideal addition to our lives, and to our thoughts.

VI. Further Exploration
Of Untalkable

This book is only the beginning, not the culmination, of an exploration of Untalkable. As an introduction, it sets out the idea with only enough discussion to understand what it is not and therefore what it might be, with some suggestions how to become more aware of it, and the possible effects and benefits of that awareness. In the best case, Untalkable rescues the aspect of the world that can't be talked about from the "either/or" choice of being kept in total secrecy, or being talked about in vague and obscure ways.

Thus we leave open the door to explore further the relation of Untalkable to the world we know, to ourselves as humans, to our lives and to our endeavors. It will be interesting to examine how this newly freed concept can

relate to the aspects of human life that open us up to Untalkable: Love, friendship, sex, nature, music, art, poetry, prayer, meditation, healing arts, pets and houseplants, philosophy, spirituality, mysticism and metaphysics, dancing, martial arts, even exercise and sports, and so on.

It will also be interesting to see how Untalkable might relate to the essentially talkable aspects of human life: science, mathematics, law, economics, business, literature and theater, education, news, television, Internet, and so forth.

I look forward to these explorations, and I welcome everyone to join the discussion:

"UNTALKABLE"
www.Untalkable.com

UNTALKABLE

Postscript

I find it fascinating that we have overlooked "what can't be talked about" for all this time, while experiencing it every day. Sooner or later we will have to give it its due, to recognize Untalkable for what it is. Then perhaps we will have succeeded in giving it a home among us, as Shakespeare long ago proposed:

> *The poet's eye, in a fine frenzy rolling,*
> *Doth glance from heaven to earth,*
>   *from earth to heaven,*
> *And as imagination bodies forth*
> *The forms of things unknown, the*
>   *poet's pen*
> *Turns them to shapes, and gives to*
>   *airy nothing*
> *A local habitation and a name.*

And perhaps the name we give it will be Untalkable.

About the Author

"Talby" is the author's childhood nickname, reflecting the simplicity and openness of Untalkable. After 45 years of thinking, reading and studying all things spiritual, he put his international career on hold to follow the succession of thoughts that eventually led to Untalkable.

Talby lives on Camano Island, Washington State, in the rainshadow of the Olympic Mountains.

UNTALKABLE

Made in the USA
San Bernardino, CA
28 October 2016